This book begins with a tribute to a deer who was killed by a hunter. It is written in an unusual format with spaces between lines, meant to give the reader pause to reflect. The book includes beautiful color photos, and brings the reader close to the sadness that both deer, and the people who love them, go through, especially during the hunting season. It also depicts two personal cases of two households who lost the deer they befriended, to hunters. In addition to sharing the experience of a summer alongside a family of deer, the book includes several rare historical photos from the Florida State Photo Collections. This is a must read for anyone who appreciates the beauty, splendor, and innocence of one of nature's most loving and beautiful residents.

Dedication

This book is dedicated to the deer that I found dead at the end of the street.

Deer at the End of the Street

I saw her at the end of my street. She lay at the edge of the clearing, where the bushes met a log, and formed a peaceful leaf strewn canopy.

There she lay, lifeless, head turned to the side, in a patch of forgotten weeds.

Beside her, and with a beer can on her head, lay a discarded empty six pack of soda pop, thrown away, just like her.

She was magnificently beautiful, but words describing this deer could not do her justice.

Her large, soft, beautiful brown eyes, looking up, and her long, thick, eyelashes, told me a story.

It was a story, of her, and her life, and the years that she struggled for existence.

It seemed she had survived many long years, in the woods.

By long years, I mean searching for water, and searching for food, maybe pausing by the sumac, for the raspberries to ripen.

Maybe she was joyous at having given birth, for the very first time.

I sat next to the log, and watched her. But, I could not snap a photo of her.

She was, soulfully, too very, beautiful, so blatantly unworthy, of the stillness.

The years had added a layer of brown velvet upon her.

I wanted to stroke her soft fur, reach out to her, tell her that I was sorry, that her life was cut short, and that her life as she knew it, was over. But,

I could not.

The next morning I returned.

The leaves around and beneath her were still dry and withered.

She was then, as she had been, untouched, except there were small deer prints around the soft earth surrounding her.

Perhaps the prints were from her offspring, standing, and waiting at dawn, for her to awaken.

I can only guess at how long they waited. Perhaps they waited there for hours.

Perhaps they were hoping for her usual companionship with them, to find water and fresh grass.

Perhaps they did not understand why she lay there without breathing.

The sun was beginning to set beneath the hills, and I did not want to stay long to see her again.

I bent down and removed the empty can of beer from her face.

I brushed off some dew from her soft coat.

Her big beautiful eyes haunted my heart.

I heard a robin call, from the distance, then turned, and walked down the path, towards home.

I imagined that she, too, would have wanted to get up, then, and go home, perhaps, to her herd, or perhaps on another daily jaunt to find water at the brook.

But, there she lay, for good, and forever, to become a part of the earth where she came from. Perhaps she was once a fawn born to a deer beyond the east side of the hill.

Perhaps she did not know her mother.

And perhaps she had never tasted a wild raspberry.

Or, perhaps she had spent many days and hours enjoying them, and blackberries, I did not know.

I did not know if she had run from hunter's guns on many occasions.

I did not know whether she had heard the call of the red tailed hawk, or seen a wild turkey, or played with any other deer.

Perhaps, she had a favorite that she romped with.

Perhaps she had stood on the sidelines once, and heard children laughing and dogs barking, in the distance.

I did not know if she had ever seen the moon.

I did not know of her life.

I only knew what she became in the end, a mere discard.

And, I wondered about her fate. She was, just yesterday, filled with life.

And now as the one I saw before me, had become a lifeless, inanimate, form, still dressed, beautifully, in her winter coat.

I visited her, on 3 more occasions. But I could not bring myself, at any of these times, to snap a photo.

On the last time I visited, I spoke to her remains.

I had to speak to what was left, because her face, was gone.

And, I thought of how many thought nothing, I suppose, of who was once there.

My Summer with Deer

Although I had not known it, this would be my joyous summer with the deer.

It was a day in June that I looked out my window one morning, to see something that I had never seen before.

Beyond my front yard, and up on the grassy hill, I saw what looked like brown spots, in the distance.

As my eyes settled in, I saw that the spots, were slowly moving forward.

The dots became larger, and as I settled in to see the image, it suddenly appeared to me that these moving brown spots were taking form in the shape of large images, and soon revealed they were deer.

And, close behind deer, I saw another, and then another, like a line, they formed a pathway down the hill, spread out as if in a large triangle, of brown, moving masses with eyes that shined.

I looked past the bushes to see yet another deer, and then to the left, beside a tree, yet another appeared.

All in all, breathless, and much beside myself with joyful emotion, I counted 18 lovely, peaceful, graceful, beautiful deer of all sizes, from 2 smaller ones to 15 large deer, moving, ever so slowly, down the hill.

And now the sight became clear to me, some with their heads down, some with their heads up, some facing the wind, some tails waving in the breeze, stealth I like and cautious, yet continuous, all grazing slowly down my hill towards my window.

I think, perhaps, I have never seen such a moving and beautiful sight. This was the beginning of my summer with deer.

Many days from then on, I watched the deer from my window. They seemed to appear more at dusk and sometimes just after dinner time.

Sometimes only ten would come down from the hill, sometimes only a trickle of three, but often, a herd of eighteen or so would start at the top of the peak, and then mozy down to the lone apple tree at the left side, near the bottom of the hill.

There, some of them would search for some apples, while the others would graze nearby, picking up their lovely heads, and perking their ears this way and that.

It was the month of June that I first noticed them.

And, in July and August, they caught a glimpse of me, watching them.

September came, and the leaves were beginning to turn.

Sometimes, upon seeing them, I would go out and walk a bit up the hill, to marvel at their grace, see them from afar, and twice, I shook down some of the hard to reach, apples from the tree.

One doe in particular would seem to let her eyes meet mine.

She did not wait much longer than a short glance, but just enough of a time to elicit an understanding, that she and I and them, were there, in appreciation and understanding, and I loved her for it.

I loved her because she graced me with her company, and because she was everything I wasn't, free, loving, and pure.

She, and her fawn nearby, and group of pausing deer, were still, in a moment in ever flowing time.

The apple tree was old, and the apples, often wormy.

The deer often struggled to reach the topmost fruit. They seemed grateful, judging by their expressions, at finding the occasional ripe apple on the ground.

It was then that I learned how hard it was for them, to find water, because after they finished eating, I watched them, go up the hill towards the only nearby small creek.

I had been to that creek often on walks, and I knew that in the summer, it often ran dry.

They knew me by my jacket.

Often, I would leave my house, and they would stand in the distance, watching me.

I saw them watching, and waiting.

A tree limb moving, would be enough to startle some.

Slowly, our eyes met, but some of the young ones continued munching on grass, and others, some older deer, turned cautiously around.

They often waited...

They knew I was their friend. I wondered if they had a message.

What were they trying to tell me? Did they want to show me something? I assumed they would leave after I left.

But hours went by, and several hours later, when I returned, they were still there waiting.

Why had the deer waited for me? Were they just being friendly with me, as they are with one another?

Always, seeing the deer brought me nothing but awe, peace, and joy.

But, I was naive to think the summer with deer would not end.

Hunting Season

The cool air of autumn was beginning to settle on the hills.

The leaves were turning, and the apple tree was near spent of its fruit.

It was a Saturday morning when I suddenly awoke at 5 a.m. to the sound of a gunshot.

I frantically grabbed onto my clothing and barely, my slippers, and ran out the door.

I heard another shot. Where was it coming from?

I turned left and looked down the road. I saw nothing.

I looked up to the upper left, and saw nothing. And then, I heard yet another shot.

My heart leaped out of my chest for that moment. I had no idea which direction to run.

I imagined that a hunter was shooting at the deer I had enjoyed and called my own.

Perhaps there were many hunters shooting at many deer.

My heart sped up and I could not breathe yet my heart, was breaking.

I imagined they were shooting at the young deer with the long ears that I had named Skipper. I imagined they had shot doe that have been so friendly to me.

Were they really going to kill his mother? Where was I to go and whatever could I do to protect them?

I felt helpless, and lost, like a mother whose children are dying.

I felt overcome by grief, and soon, the feeling turned to anger and then rage.

It was hunting season. That's what had come upon me, and them.

I heard shots from the hills at different times. Each time I heard one, I imagined one of my precious deer, falling.

Was it the one with the beautiful golden coat? Was it the one who always gazed at me?

Was she in pain? Was she frightened, as anyone would be?

Would I ever see her again? Was it the young buck?

Was it one of the three who watched me get into the car? Was it the one who pawed at all the apples?

Or was it the one who chose to pick the apples off the highest branch? The 3 weeks of hunting season were torture for me.

The day hunting season finally ended, it felt like an eternity had gone by. I waited for the deer.

But, I did not see any. It was early morning, and as I leaned on my window ledge.

I saw the sun rise, and I saw no moving deer. Days passed, and each morning and evening I looked for them.

I gazed out my window, looking for my deer friends. I saw birds flying on occasion.

I saw the leafless trees. There were some blue jays chattering in the corner tree, and I saw children on their way to school. But, I saw no deer.

Weeks and weeks went by, and I still saw nothing but the ordinary quiet street.
There were no deer to greet me, anymore, when I walked down the road.

There were no deer on the hill, nor by the apple tree, and there were no deer anywhere to be seen.

I tried to console myself into believing that the deer had merely run for safety, and they were safe somewhere else, maybe surviving in the woods.

But my voice echoed inwardly to the sad truth, that the deer were gone.

Many times for many months, I glanced out the window, and saw the hillside as it had been before, green, but now lifeless.
I walked down the street, many times throughout the upcoming seasons. I had a feeling of loss and emptiness that often came and settled upon me.

One year passed.

In early May one morning, the following year, the one, crooked apple tree at the bottom of the hill, was beginning its yearly bloom.

I wondered if any deer would ever have a chance to enjoy those apples again.

I wondered if I would ever see a deer, with her soft brown eyes, look up at me, ever again.

And I asked myself, if one magically appeared, if a few had escaped the hunter's gunfire, how would I feel, then, knowing what I know now, that deer are targets for hunters, and her life would only end the next hunting season?

The shade, the sun,
the trees, the barren, leaf strewn floor,
the silent empty quiet
of the deer that are no more.
I hear whispers in the twilight
I hear spirits in the night
- (the deer) but the beauty that once engulfed me
has vanished from my sight.

The trees are filled with acorns now and the flowers
are everywhere
but the deer that used to greet me sweetly, none of
them are there.
The hills reflect the deepest hues
the field is filled with green and, near the hill, a paler
yellow flower
but those deer I used to watch and love,
have breathed their final hour.

That startled hoof, their sweet repose, a head tossed
to and fro
the ears that used to bend and sway, when gentle
winds would blow
I miss them now, as I missed them then
as they once missed each other
when a doe fell, shattered,
or her sister or his brother.

I watch, now, as the sun goes down and sifts the
dawn, today
it reminds me so of spotted fawns that used to, jump
and play.
The barren field, the empty path

It cuts me to the core

And now I cry, for that empty place, and the deer that are no more.
the hunters came, their killing season, with bait, and guns
their faces etched like stone
they killed them all, one by one,
in the field, which was their home.
The barren field, that empty path it cuts me to the core
and now I mourn, for that empty place, and the deer that are no more.

Fawns to buck, why them?

This fawn, one of two born in May, will only have two more months with her mother, as hunting season will then begin.

The three of them came down today, the mother and her two babies. The mother deer seems so proud of her offspring. They were frolicking around with each other, and my thoughts turned to what lies ahead for those two fawns, when they are left as orphans, to fend for themselves.

This fawn is only a few months and small with spots.....from fawn, to buck, why oh why, them?

Sad endings for other deer

The following images, with captions, are written by a friend, in memory of a deer named Jasper.

Jasper as a yearling

My daughter, Gracie, petting Jasper.

Jasper eating oats. Some are stuck to her nose.

Gracie giving Jasper apples.

Jasper's son.

Jasper and her son.

Jasper and her daughter.

Jasper would come up on the deck with her fawn to my glass sliding door.

She was a friend who I loved so much and who loved me. She was murdered the last day of hunting season 2007.

Prince & Baby Metz

Prince and Baby Metz were friendly deer who often visited our yard. The following photos were sent in as a tribute to them.

Baby Metz was born in our yard. His mother was killed by a hunter.

Older Baby Metz

The Prince 6-19-02

Prince was killed by hunters in a neighbor's yard

Handsome Prince

The life of deer in images

Deer struggle to keep warm during winter.

Deer in winter often struggle for food.

It is hard for them to find water, when cold weather freezes creeks.

Deer form a deep connection with their families.

Often, deer end up alone, and lonely, after hunting season.

Deer show tender affection to other animals.

Deer have been respected and revered throughout history.

Friendly and cheerful young doe.

Callous Disregard for a life - hunters and poachers

Of the millions of deer that are killed by hunters, each year, many are does, thus mothers, leaving many fawns to become orphans.